ULTIMATE ANIMAL DEFENSES

TOOTH AND NAIL
DEADLY JAWS AND CLAWS

Gareth Stevens
PUBLISHING

BY AGATHA GREGSON

Please visit our website, www.garethstevens.com. For a free color catalog of all our high-quality books, call toll free 1-800-542-2595 or fax 1-877-542-2596.

Library of Congress Cataloging-in-Publication Data

Gregson, Agatha, author.
Tooth and nail : deadly jaws and claws / Agatha Gregson.
pages cm. — (Ultimate animal defenses)
Includes bibliographical references and index.
ISBN 978-1-4824-4446-9 (pbk.)
ISBN 978-1-4824-4387-5 (6 pack)
ISBN 978-1-4824-4428-5 (library binding)
1. Predation (Biology)—Juvenile literature. 2. Predatory animals—Juvenile literature. 3. Animal weapons—Juvenile literature. 4. Animal defenses—Juvenile literature. 5. Animal behavior—Juvenile literature. I. Title.
QL758.G744 2017
591.5'3—dc23

2015021549

First Edition

Published in 2017 by
Gareth Stevens Publishing
111 East 14th Street, Suite 349
New York, NY 10003

Designer: Katelyn E. Reynolds
Editor: Therese Shea

Photo credits: Cover, p. 1 Purestock/Getty Images; cover, pp. 1–24 (background texture) vector illustration/Shutterstock.com; p. 5 (bald eagle) Critterbiz/Shutterstock.com; p. 5 (crocodile) Volodymyr Burdiak/Shutterstock.com; p. 5 (shark) Elsa Hoffmann/Shutterstock.com; p. 5 (lion) adennis26win/Shutterstock.com; p. 7 MattiaATH/Shutterstock.com; p. 9 Marc Herrmann/Shutterstock.com; p. 11 Roger de Montfort/Shutterstock.com; p. 12 Neale Cousland/Shutterstock.com; p. 13 Thomas Dressler/Gallo Images/Getty Images; p. 15 Kevin Frates/Moment Open/Getty Images; p. 17 (inset) kerstiny/Shutterstock.com; p. 17 (main) Universal Images Group/Getty Images; p. 19 (inset) S.J. Krasemann/Photolibrary/Getty Images; p. 19 (main) Patrick Endres/Design Pics/First Light/Getty Images; p. 20 Gustavocarra/Wikimedia Commons; p. 21 (bear) yui/Shutterstock.com; p. 21 (owl) Chris Humphries/Shutterstock.com; p. 21 (ostrich) Rafal Cichawa/Shutterstock.com; p. 21 (snapping turtle) Andrea J Smith/Shutterstock.com.

Printed in the United States of America

CPSIA compliance information: Batch #CS16GS : For further information contact Gareth Stevens, New York, New York at 1-800-542-2595.

CONTENTS

Words in the glossary appear in **bold** type the first time they are used in the text.

PREDATOR AND PREY

When you think of predators, you probably think of scary beasts with long, sharp teeth and even longer, sharper claws. Many predators at the top of their food chain, such as lions and sharks, do have some frightening **weapons** like these.

However, there are lots of animals that have these **adaptations** to fight their enemies. Some use their teeth and claws to **defend** themselves or their families. In this book, we'll learn more about these creatures and how they fight back!

THESE PREDATORS HAVE ADAPTATIONS SUCH AS KNIFE-SHARP TEETH AND POINTED CLAWS THAT HELP THEM STAY AT THE TOP OF THEIR FOOD CHAINS.

BABOONS BITE

Baboons are large monkeys that live in Africa and the western **Arabian Peninsula**. They're very smart, often noisy, and sometimes **ferocious**. Baboons stand out among monkeys for the incredible size of their **canine** teeth. These teeth can be 2 inches (5 cm) long. That's longer than the teeth of most sharks!

You might think baboons use their teeth to hunt. Actually, they use them to both fight and defend themselves in their own herd. Male baboons may battle their herd leader as well as other males to find a **mate**.

SO WILD!

Sometimes, baboons show each other the size of their teeth instead of fighting!

BABOONS ARE OMNIVOROUS, WHICH MEANS THEY EAT BOTH PLANTS AND ANIMALS.

WATCH OUT FOR WOLVES

Wolves are mighty predators. They can run for miles tracking a meal. When they find prey, they take it down with their powerful jaws, which are strong enough to crush bone! When in packs, wolves can kill much larger animals than themselves, such as moose.

However, wolves may use their deadly adaptations on each other. Wolves guard their hunting territory. When other wolves enter this territory, they may attack each other, biting and tearing until there's a winner.

SO WILD!

Wolves may also battle to become leader of their pack.

WOLVES CAN BE FOUND IN ASIA, EUROPE, AND NORTH AMERICA. ONLY TWO SPECIES, OR KINDS, OF WOLVES REMAIN TODAY: THE GRAY, OR TIMBER, WOLF AND THE RED WOLF.

GROUNDHOGS ON GUARD

Groundhogs, also called woodchucks, are the largest members of the squirrel family. They live in North America. Groundhogs are herbivores, which means they eat plants, fruits, roots, and stems, but no meat.

Groundhogs usually live alone in a deep, long den they dig themselves. However, they have to come up to eat. Groundhogs are slow, which makes them a target for quick predators such as foxes and raccoons. If a groundhog can't get back to its den, it uses its sharp teeth for **protection**.

SO WILD!

Like the teeth of other **rodents**, groundhog teeth never stop growing!

GROUNDHOGS ALSO USE THEIR TEETH TO **WHISTLE** TO OTHER GROUNDHOGS, WARNING THEM OF DANGER.

HAZARDOUS HIPPO

The hippopotamus, or hippo, is an herbivore. However, it's also considered to be the most dangerous large animal in Africa! How can this be?

Hippos are huge! They may grow to be 5 feet (1.5 m) tall and 14 feet (4.3 m) long. They can weigh 4 tons (3.6 mt). When hippos think something or someone is a **threat** to themselves or their children, they **charge**. They can run more than 20 miles (32 km) per hour. They may also bite with their giant canine teeth.

SO WILD!

Each of a hippo's always-growing canine teeth can weigh 6.5 pounds (3 kg)!

HIPPOS SHOW THEIR TEETH WHEN THEY'RE READY TO FIGHT.

RISKY RED PANDAS

The red panda of East Asia is much smaller than the giant panda. Red pandas are usually no longer than 26 inches (66 cm), with a tail about another 19 inches (48 cm) long.

Red pandas have supersharp claws to climb trees, where they sleep during the day. At night, their powerful jaws and pointy teeth are perfect for chomping on **bamboo**. However, they also help these animals protect themselves from their predators, especially snow leopards. Red pandas may stand on their back legs and strike predators with their front paws.

RED PANDAS LOOK A BIT LIKE RACCOONS WITH REDDISH OR BROWNISH FUR.

KILLER CASSOWARY KICKS

The strange-looking cassowary is often called the most dangerous bird in the world. This large, flightless bird is so deadly because of a talon, or curved claw, on each of its feet. Each talon can be 4 inches (10 cm) long. With a powerful kicking motion, this creature can slice open an animal easily!

Cassowaries eat fruits, bugs, spiders, and small animals. They don't have any real predators except for humans, who eat them. However, they've been known to attack and even kill people they think are a threat.

CASSOWARIES HAVE A HORNY GROWTH ON THEIR HEAD CALLED A CASQUE (KASK).

SO WILD!

Southern cassowaries of Australia and New Guinea are the largest of the three species. They can be 5 feet (1.5 m) tall.

MOOSE ON THE MOVE

Moose are the largest members of the deer family. Also called elk, they live in northern parts of North America, Europe, and Asia. Moose can be 7 feet (2 m) tall at the shoulder and weigh more than 1,000 pounds (454 kg)! Still, moose have to defend themselves against hungry predators such as bears and wolves.

Plant-eating moose don't use teeth and claws to protect themselves, but they do use their dangerous pointed hooves. A single powerful kick from a moose can easily kill one of their ferocious predators!

THIS MOOSE DEFENDS HER YOUNG FROM WOLVES IN ALASKA.

SO WILD!

A hoof is made of keratin, the matter that makes up your nails. However, a hoof is much thicker and harder.

HORRIFYING HAIRY FROGS

The hairy frog, sometimes called the horror frog, has a pretty gross adaptation. It has clawlike bones within its back legs. When the frog is attacked, it can force the sharp bones to poke through its skin so the creature can use the bones like claws! Scientists don't know if the frog's skin grows back around the bones after the attack or not.

Look at the next page to learn even more amazing defensive adaptations. Just make sure none of these animals ever think *you're* a threat!

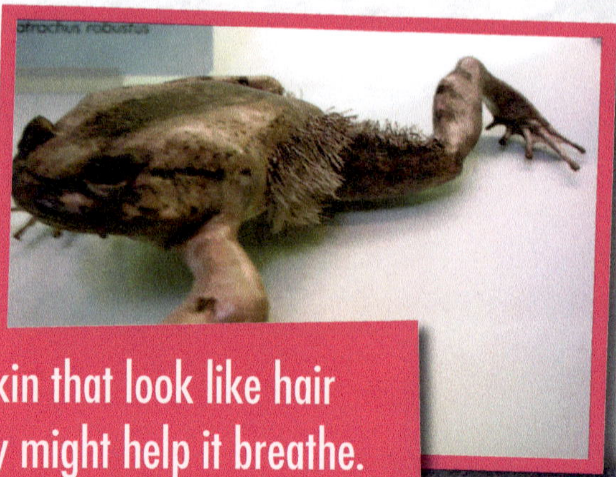

The hairy frog grows bits of skin that look like hair around its legs and back. They might help it breathe.

JAWS, CLAWS, AND MORE

A bear swipes at threats with long, sharp claws.

An owl uses curved talons and a sharp beak to rip apart predators.

DEFENSIVE ADAPTATIONS

An ostrich has long talons and a kick powerful enough to kill lions.

A snapping turtle uses snapping jaws and thick claws to attack enemies.

GLOSSARY

adaptation: a change in a type of animal that makes it better able to live in its surroundings

Arabian Peninsula: a land in the southwestern part of Asia that is surrounded on three sides by water

bamboo: a giant grass with long hollow stems that grows in warm, wet areas

canine: a long, pointed tooth near the front of the mouth

charge: to attack by rushing forward

defend: to guard against an enemy

ferocious: fierce and wild

mate: one of two animals that come together to produce babies

protection: the act of keeping something safe

rodent: a small, furry animal with large front teeth, such as a mouse or rat

threat: something likely to cause harm

weapon: something used to fight an enemy

whistle: to make a sound by blowing breath through lips or teeth

FOR MORE INFORMATION

BOOKS

Riehecky, Janet. *Teeth, Claws, and Jaws: Animal Weapons and Defenses*. North Mankato, MN: Capstone Press, 2012.

Rissman, Rebecca. *Claws*. Chicago, IL: Heinemann Library, 2011.

Stout, Frankie. *Nature's Nastiest Biters*. New York, NY: PowerKids Press, 2008.

WEBSITES

Facts: All About Predators
idahoptv.org/sciencetrek/topics/predators/facts.cfm
Find out more about the adaptations of both predators and prey.

Top 10 Animal Adaptations
www.animalplanet.com/wild-animals/animal-adaptations/
Read about some other adaptations that have helped animals survive in the wild.

INDEX